max science primary

Workbook 5

DISCOVERING THROUGH ENQUIRY

LAWRIE RYAN

SERIES EDITOR: **BOB KIBBLE**

macmillan education

INTERNATIONAL CURRICULUM

Macmillan Education
4 Crinan Street
London N1 9XW
A division of Springer Nature Limited

Companies and representatives throughout the world

Workbook ISBN 978-1-380-02168-7

First published 2019

Original design by EMC Design Ltd and Macmillan Education
Page make-up by Ink Design
Illustrated by Alistair Ackermann, Deevine Design, Natalie and Tamsin Hinrichsen, Ilias Arahovitis, Martin Cain, Moreno Chiacchiera and Eric Smith c/o Beehive Illustration
Alistair Ackermann pp 6, 7, 10, 20, 36; Deevine Design pp 15, 38, 80, 81, 82; Ilias Arahovitis c/o Beehive Illustration pp 8, 13, 31, 41, 53, 68, 79; Martin Cain c/o Beehive Illustration 101; Moreno Chiacchiera c/o Beehive Illustration pp 2, 61 (top & bottom), 72, 95, 109; Eric Smith c/o Beehive Illustration pp 9, 22, 27, 30, 67, 96, 111; Natalie and Tamsin Hinrichsen pp 109
Cover design by Sparks Publishing Services Ltd and Macmillan Education
Cover illustration by Star Publishing Pte Ltd and Jorge Santillan c/o Beehive Illustration Agency
Picture research by Susannah Jayes

The author and publishers would like to thank the following for permission to reproduce their photographs:
Alamy/Custom Life Science p43; **Getty Images**/amperesey p12(2), Getty Images/John Elk III p12(4), Getty Images/Martyn Goddard p107, Getty Images/Tommy Hindley/Professional Sport/Popperfoto p7, Getty Images/Kcris Ramos p12(1), Getty Images/Squareman p49; **REX Shutterstock**/Joe Castro/EPA-EFE p1; **Shutterstock**/Darren Baker p12(3); **Springer Nature Ltd**/Natalie Dawkins p56.

Printed and bound in Brazil
2022
12

Contents

Introducing the *Max Science primary* Workbook

The **Max Science primary Workbook** accompanies the **Student Book** for class and home use. All the numbered activities and extension activities found in the Student Book are expanded with clear answer spaces and support. Instructions carefully show if activities are to be done independently, in pairs or in groups.

Practising my science language

Supported activities focus on improving scientific literacy to make the learning of science through the medium of English more accessible.

Extending understanding

Extension questions encourage learners to go a bit further to improve the depth of understanding.

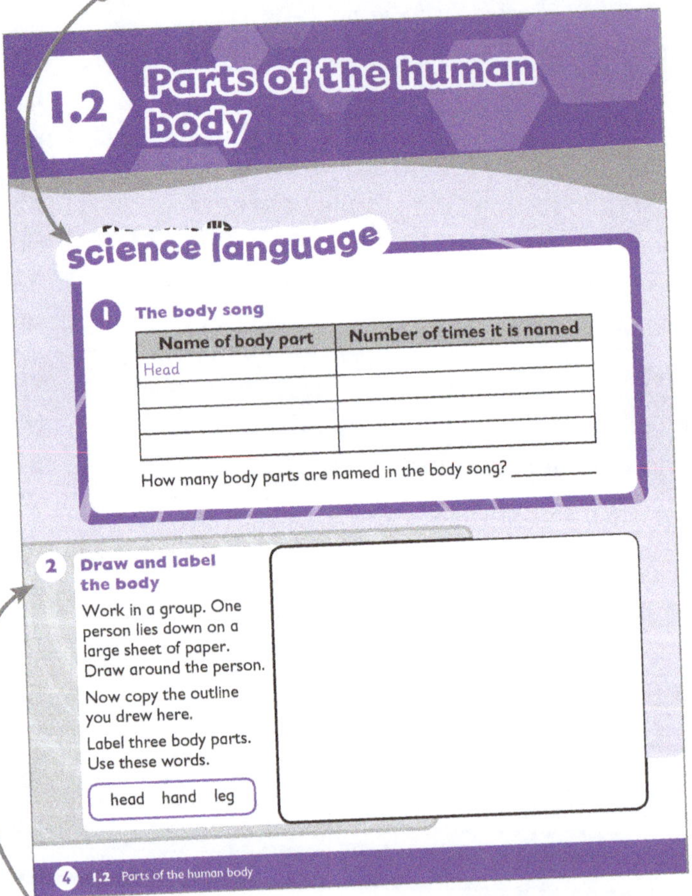

1.2 Parts of the human body

Practising my science language

1 The body song

Name of body part	Number of times it is named
Head	

How many body parts are named in the body song? ________

2 Draw and label the body

Work in a group. One person lies down on a large sheet of paper. Draw around the person.

Now copy the outline you drew here.

Label three body parts. Use these words.

head hand leg

4 1.2 Parts of the human body

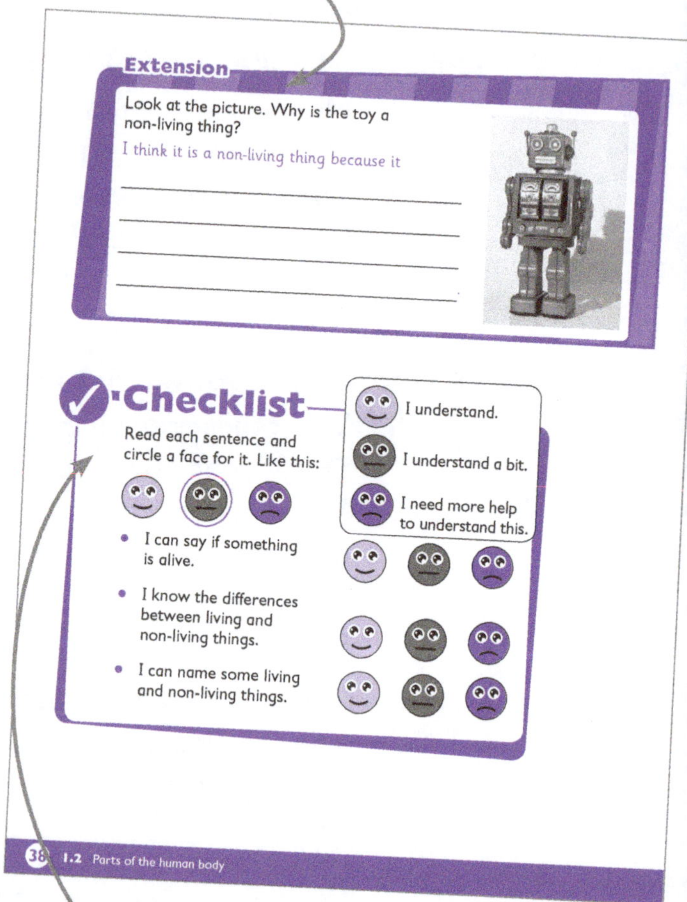

Extension

Look at the picture. Why is the toy a non-living thing?

I think it is a non-living thing because it

Checklist

Read each sentence and circle a face for it. Like this:

I understand.

I understand a bit.

I need more help to understand this.

- I can say if something is alive.
- I know the differences between living and non-living things.
- I can name some living and non-living things.

38 1.2 Parts of the human body

Exploring science further

Numbered activities from the Student Book are expanded to provide a framework for learners' answers. Learners can record their scientific progress, insights and results.

Assessing progress

End-of-topic checklists provide opportunities for learners to record what they have learnt so far.

1 The way we see things

1 Blocking light

A ball boy lowers a canopy over the tennis players when they sit down for a short rest between games.

Use these words to explain why:

sun	shade	light	shadow

The canopy is lowered to ______________________________

____

____

______________________________.

2 How do we see things?

a. Look at the picture.

Can Daniel play tennis on a dark night if this is true?

Circle your answer: **Yes** **No**

continues on following page ...

... continued from previous page

b. Finish the note to Daniel, explaining to him how seeing things works.

Dear Daniel,

I think your ideas about how we see things are wrong.

What really happens is that

____

____

____

____

____

____

____

____

____

Best wishes,

____

c. Share your ideas with other pairs. Do you all have the same ideas?

Circle your answer: **Yes** **No**

Write down one idea that is different to yours.

____

____

____

____

____

1.1 Sources of light and seeing

1 Modelling a sunny house

a. Make a cardboard model room to show a sunny house:

- Use a cardboard box as the building.
- Cut a hole in the side for a window. Only cut three sides of the window. Then you can open and close it.
- Use a torch as the Sun and a matchbox as a table inside the house.
- Fully open the window in the cardboard box to start with.

Hint

Your teacher might help you to cut the window using a sharp craft knife.

b. Darken the area around you.

What happens inside the 'house' when the torch is held in different positions? Write down your observations.

When the torch is held, ______________________________

____

____

______________________________.

c. Explain why a table in a bright room is visible to us, yet in a completely dark room we cannot see it.

We cannot see the table in a dark room because ______________________________

____

____

______________________________.

2 Comparing light sources

Work with a partner.

a. Look closely at the torch you used in Activity 1 and the photos of **light sources** on page 6 of the Student Book. Complete these sentences:

- The torch is similar to the light sources in the photos because it

  ____.

- The torch is different to the light sources in the photos because it

  ____

  and it ______________________________________.

b. Think about the direction of light from the torch.

- Why doesn't the torch give off light in all directions?

  ____

  ____

- Why is it not safe to stare straight into the light given off from the torch?

  ____

  ____

c. Name **one** other light source you should never look at directly.

____

____

Extension

Draw a diagram to show what you think happens to light when it passes from a bright light source through a pair of sunglasses, as shown in the picture.

1.2 Rays of light

Practising my science language

1 Think about shadows

a. Explain the tennis players' shadows. Use these words:

light	floodlights
opaque	block

b. What do you think will happen to the shadows if two separate floodlights at one end of the stadium are turned off?

On this picture of a tennis player, draw the shadows she will have when the two lights shown are turned off.

Extension

Why can a tennis player never run faster than their shadow?

A tennis player can never run faster than their shadow because ___________

____

____.

2 Exploring the path of light

a. Look at the picture. Why can Salim and Ravit not see each other?

They cannot see each other because ___________________________

____

____.

b. Can you think of a way to make the light change direction so Salim and Ravit can see around the corner?

What do you need to place at the corner?

To make the light change direction ___________________________

____

____.

c. Predict the path of the light and draw your idea on the picture below.

Extension

A boy can see two candles burning at the end of a table. They are 20 cm apart.

Draw a ray diagram on the picture to show how the boy can see both candles.

Checklist

I understand.

I understand a bit.

I need more help to understand this.

Read each sentence and circle a face for it. Like this:

- I know some light sources.
- I know how we can see a light source.
- I can explain how shadows are formed.
- I know that light travels in straight lines.
- I can draw rays of light on a ray diagram.

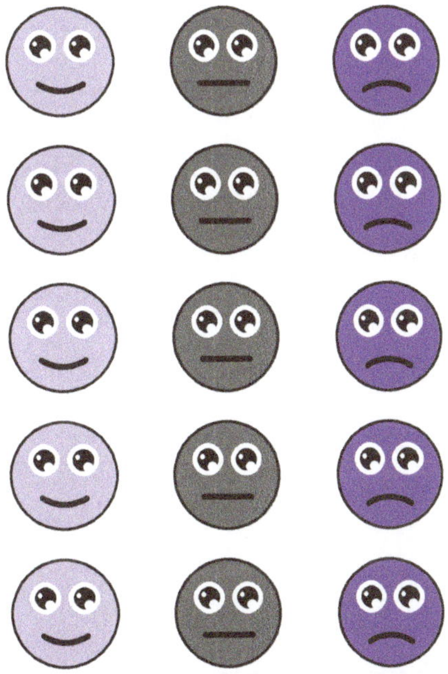

1.3 Mirrors

Practising my science language

1 Check yourself out

a. Why can you see yourself in a mirror?

I can see myself in a mirror because ________________________________

____

____.

b. Do you think the image of yourself in a mirror is still there in a totally dark room?

Circle your answer: **Yes** **No**

Explain your answer.

This is because ____

____

____

____.

2 Mirror writing

a. Here is the image of my name as seen in the mirror:

b. How can you make an image of your name that looks the same as the way you wrote it?

c. Compare a real object with its image in a mirror.

Complete the table.

How are the real object and its image *the same*?	How are the real object and its image *different*?

3 Investigating reflection

Draw a ray diagram to show the ray box and the mirror that you set up for your investigation, and the reflected light ray. Use a ruler to draw the light ray.

4 How we can use mirrors

a. Explain how the mirrors in Photos 1 to 4 are used.

b. You can write a sentence or draw a diagram on a separate piece of paper showing light rays.

Photo 1

Photo 2

Photo 3

Photo 4

5 Up periscope!

a. Why do periscopes contain **two** mirrors?

Write down your answer or draw a ray diagram.

b. Complete the picture below to show the path of a ray of light from the bird on the island to the person in the submarine.

6 Designing a periscope

Work in a small group or with a partner.

a. Draw your design for a periscope as a labelled diagram below.

Extension

A laser is a powerful and narrow beam of light. Find out one use of lasers.

We can use lasers to ______________________________

____

______________________________.

1.4 Investigating light

Practising my science language

1 Using a light meter

Work in small groups.

a. How does the brightness of light from a torch change the further away it is?

Plan a fair test, using a light meter to find the answer to the question above.

- What is the only variable you will change?

  ____

- What will you measure with the light meter?

  ____

- What will you keep the same to make it a fair test?

  To make it a fair test, I will ______________________________

  ______________________________.

After you have carried out your investigation, draw a line graph like the one here to show your results.

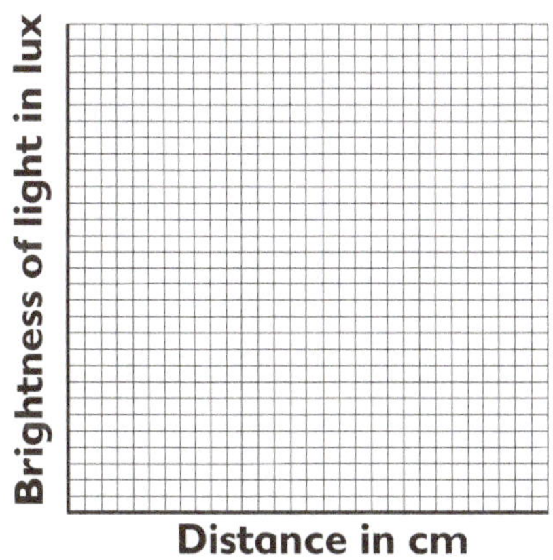

Your teacher will help you to plan your graph.

What pattern do your results show? Discuss in a small group and then complete the sentence below:

We can conclude that the nearer you are to the torch the ____________ *the light is.*

continues on following page …

... continued from previous page

b. How much light is reflected from the surface of a mirror?

Circle the correct bold option in the following sentence:

The brightness of the light reflected from a flat mirror is **higher than** / **lower than** / **the same as** the light hitting the mirror.

c. How much light passes through a piece of tracing or tissue paper?

Circle the correct bold option in the following sentence:

The brightness of the light that passes through a piece of tissue or tracing paper is **higher than** / **lower than** / **the same as** the light hitting the paper.

Practising my science language

2 Which surfaces make the best reflectors of light?

Work in pairs. Choose three different materials. Discuss the questions below and then write your answers.

a. How will you plan to make your investigation a fair test? What things (variables) will you keep the same when testing each material?

____

____

b. Put your materials in order, with the best reflector first.

____

____

c. Look back at your order of reflectors. What conclusion can you make about good and bad reflectors of light?

Materials that are good reflectors are ____________________.

Materials that are bad reflectors are ____________________.

continues on following page ...

... continued from previous page

d. Can you trust the results of your investigation and your conclusion? Explain why (or why not).

Circle the correct bold option then complete the following sentence:

We **can** / **cannot** trust the results because ______________________________

____

____.

What improvements could you make to your method? This is your evaluation.

If we did the investigation again, we could make it better by measuring ____________________ instead of ____________________

____.

3 **A bright classroom**

Work in small groups.

a. Draw your design for a bright classroom in the box below.

Label the materials you chose.

b. Explain to a partner how each of your choices will make the classroom as bright as possible in natural light.

Extension

Draw a sketch to show how you would use a light meter in your investigation for Activity 2. (Which surfaces make the best reflectors of light?) Draw the light meter as a small box.

Checklist

- I understand.
- I understand a bit.
- I need more help to understand this.

Read each sentence and circle a face for it. Like this:

I understand.	I understand a bit.	I need more help to understand this.
	(circled)	

- I can show how rays of light can be reflected by surfaces.
- I know how we can see a reflection of an object.
- I can describe some uses of mirrors.
- I can describe and explain what makes a good reflector of light.
- I can investigate the brightness of light and its reflection.

Glossary

Fill in the meaning of these words in your own language.

beam

eyes

image

light

light source

mirror

object

opaque

ray

ray diagram

reflect

shadow

surface

translucent

transparent

2 Evaporation and condensation

Practising my science language

1 Linking key words

a. What do we call water when it is solid?

____

What do we call the water that rises from a kettle of boiling water as a gas?

____

b. Draw a mind map to link the following words.

Put labelled arrows between the words you choose to link:

water steam liquid ice gas solid

c. Is your partner's mind map similar or different?

continues on following page ...

... continued from previous page

d. Amira wants to make links between more words. She suggests:

kettle pour drip cold

- Draw a new mind map to show the connections you can find between these words.
- Can you add some more words of your own?

2 Modelling solids, liquids and gases

After discussing your human 'models of matter', make a table to show:

- the good points
- the bad points.

Good points	Bad points

2.1 Evaporation

1 Where do all the puddles go?

a. What happens to the size of a puddle when the Sun comes out?

- Complete the sentence below to write your prediction.

When the Sun comes out the puddle will get ______________________

______________________.

- Explain **why** you think this will happen.

This will happen because ______________________

______________________.

b. Write a plan to find out how quickly a puddle changes. You have a measuring tape and a stop clock.

Our plan

What should we measure with the measuring tape?

____

How often should we make our measurements?

____

How can we make sure our measurements are taken across the same part of the water each time?

____

continues on following page ...

... continued from previous page

c. What type of graph is best to show the pattern of your results?

Tick the graph you will use: ☐ **bar chart** ☐ **line graph**

Explain your choice of graph. Fill in the gaps in the sentence below.

I will use a ____________________ because both variables, the ____________________ across the water and the ____________________ from our first measurement, are shown as numbers.

Practising my

science language

Extension

a. Carry out your investigation from Activity 1.

b. Record your measurements in the table.

Our results

Time in hours	Distance across the water's surface in cm
0	

c. Interpret your results and write your conclusion.

Our conclusion

From our results we found that ____

____

____

____.

2 Warming water

a. Watch your teacher heat a pan of water on a hot plate.

What do you notice, or observe, above the water **before** it boils?

Before the water boils, I can see ______________________________

____

______________________________.

b. Explain this observation. Use the word '**particles**' in your explanation.

I can see this because ______________________________

____

____

______________________________.

3 That smells nice!

Watch your teacher warm some scented oil (oil containing perfume) using a tealight candle.

a. Who smells the oil first? ______________

b. What do you notice about their position in the room?

____

c. Write about what happens in the room as the oil warms up. Include details about the particles, the air and the perfume.

As the oil warms up ______________________________

____

____

____

______________________________.

Practising my

science language

4 What makes washing dry more quickly?

Work in a small group.

a. Discuss the factors (variables) that affect how quickly washing will dry. Write your ideas here.

The washing will dry more quickly if ______________________

____

____.

b. Circle the variable that you will investigate.

c. Plan a fair test to see how your chosen variable affects the time it takes your washing to dry.

Our plan

Which variables will you keep the same in each test?

How will you do this?

The variables I will keep the same are ______________

____

How will you judge how quickly the washing is drying?

____

d. Record your observations by completing the table.

Our results

continues on following page …

... continued from previous page

e. Analyse your results and write your conclusion. Make sure you mention 'evaporation'.

Our conclusion

We found out that ______________________________

____

______________________________.

f. How could you make the results more reliable?

Complete the sentence:

We could make our results more reliable by r______________ the tests more than once.

Extension

Look at the two ways to hang washing out to dry on page 26 of the Student Book.

Mrs Khanduri used to hang her washing on a long line. Then she bought a new rotary drier.

a. The washing dried faster on the old, long line. Discuss with a partner and then explain why.

The washing dried faster on the long line because ______________

____

______________________________.

b. What is the advantage of the rotary drier?

The advantage of the rotary drier is ______________

____

______________________________.

2.2 Condensation

Practising my science language

1 Talking about condensation

a. Look at the cartoon. Which idea do you agree with?

I agree that ____________

____

______________________.

b. Explain why you think this is the best idea.

I think this is the best idea because ______________________

____

______________________.

2 Observing condensation

a. What do you observe when your teacher boils a kettle of water and holds a mirror above its spout?

Complete the sentence:

When the steam hits the mirror ______________________

____

______________________.

continues on following page ...

... continued from previous page

b) Explain what happens on the surface of the mirror. Write about the 'particles of water' and the changing temperature.

Complete the sentence:

This happens because ______________________________

______________________________.

Practising my science language

3 Surface temperature affects condensation

Why is there more condensation on a cold mirror than on a warm mirror?

Complete the words in the sentence:

This happens because more p__________ of water cool down on the c__________ mirror than on the w__________ mirror.

Practising my science language

Extension

Work in pairs.

a. What does 'evaporation' mean? Write down the definition.

____

____

b. What does 'condensation' mean? Write down the definition.

____

____

c. Produce a labelled drawing on the next page to help you explain both evaporation and condensation.

continues on following page ...

... continued from previous page

Checklist

Read each sentence and circle a face for it. Like this:

🙂	I understand.
😐	I understand a bit.
🙁	I need more help to understand this.

- I can describe what "evaporation" and "condensation" mean.
- I can list some examples of evaporation and condensation.
- I can describe what happens to the particles in a liquid when it evaporates.
- I can investigate and understand what affects the drying of clothes on a washing line.
- I can describe what happens to the particles in a gas when the gas condenses.

2.3 The water cycle

1 Clouds

Work in small groups.

Ling and her friends have some ideas about clouds. Do you agree with them?

Ideas I **agree** with:

Ideas I **disagree** with:

Ideas I'm **not sure** about:

2 Flow diagram water cycle

Look at the diagram of the water cycle on pages 30–31 of the Student Book.

Organise the changes in the state of matter of water in the water cycle into a simple flow diagram.

Water in the sea

(start here)

3 Daniel's bathtime

Compare the water cycle in nature to Daniel's bathtime. Can the water cycle happen in Daniel's bathroom?

I think that the water cycle ______________________

____

____

____

____

____

______________________________________.

Practising my
science language

4 Does the surface area affect how fast water evaporates?

Work in a small group.

a. Draw the four different-shaped containers in your investigation. Label them A, B, C and D.

b. Make a prediction about what will happen to the water. From which container will water evaporate fastest?

Our prediction

Put the containers in order (with the one with the fastest evaporation first).

1st: ____________________ 2nd: ____________________

3rd: ____________________ 4th: ____________________

Explain your choice of order.

I put the containers in this order because ____________________

____

____________________.

continues on following page …

... continued from previous page

c. Plan your investigation.

Our plan

How will you make this a fair test? Write down the variables you will keep the same.

We will keep these variables the same:

____

____

How will you measure how much water has evaporated after a set time?

We will measure ______________________________

____

____

d. Fill in the missing header and record your results in the table.

Our results

Label of container	
A	
B	
C	
D	

Draw a graph of your results on the next page.

Hint

Remember: We use a bar chart when we describe the variable changed between tests (the independent variable) with words or labels.

continues on following page ...

... continued from previous page

continues on following page ...

... continued from previous page

e. Look back at your results. Was the prediction you made correct?

Our conclusion

Using your measurements, put the containers in order again (with the one with the fastest evaporation first).

1st: ____________________ 2nd: ____________________

3rd: ____________________ 4th: ____________________

Circle your answer: My predicted order was correct / incorrect.

Extension

Look at the 'Changes of state' flow diagrams on page 33 of the Student Book.

How can you start each flow diagram with water in its **solid** state?

Fill in the missing words:

Water in a cold sea can exist in its solid state as ____________________.

This often floats in large blocks or slabs called ____________________.

Checklist

Read each sentence and circle a face for it.
Like this:

- I understand.
- I understand a bit.
- I need more help to understand this.

I can describe the water cycle that occurs in nature.	☺	😐	☹
I can explain the stages of the water cycle, including any changes of state.	☺	😐	☹
I can use the idea of water particles when explaining the water cycle.	☺	😐	☹

2.4 Changing the state of water

1 Cooking food and making drinks

a. Make a list of foods that you boil in water before eating.

____

____

____

b. Which drinks are made with boiling water?

____

____

c. Why is boiling water used to make these drinks rather than cold water?

These drinks are made with boiling water because ______________________

____

____.

2 Observing boiling water

Watch your teacher heat a pan of water until it starts to boil.

a. What do you see happening as the water boils?

As the water starts to boil I see ______________________

____

____

____.

b. Write down the boiling point of water. _____ °C

Practising my

science language

3 Melting ice

Work in pairs.

a. Write down the melting point of ice. ______ °C

b. What is the freezing point of water? ______ °C

c. What is happening to the water particles in the ice cubes as the ice melts?

Complete this answer:

The water particles in **solid** ice are fixed in position in regular patterns. As the ice melts ____

____.

4 What happens to the temperature of water as it is heated?

a. Record the temperature of water as it is heated to its boiling point at the time intervals in the table:

Time in minutes	Temperature in °C
0	
2	
4	
6	
8	
10	

If the water does not boil in 10 minutes, extend your table.

b. What happened to the temperature once the water started to boil?

____

5 Drawing line graphs

Copy the axes onto graph paper. Complete the graph to show your results from Activity 4.

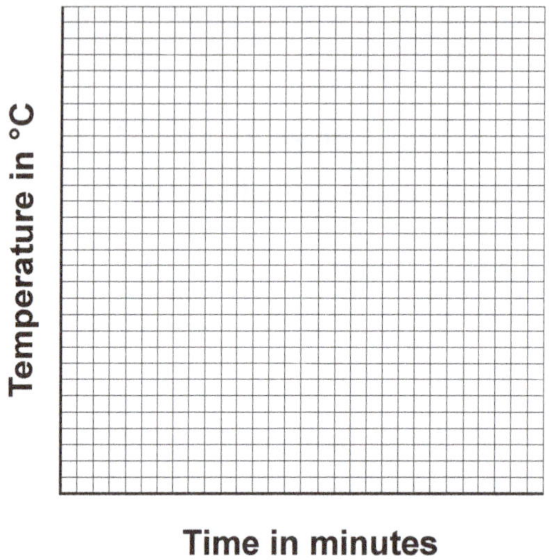

Extension

Look at the line graph on page 38 of the Student Book.

a. What was the water temperature after five minutes? ____ °C

b. What was the temperature of the room at the start of the experiment? ____ °C

Explain how you worked this out.

____

c. How long did it take for the water to boil? ____ minutes

d. Was the water heated steadily as the temperature was rising?

Circle the answer: **Yes** **No**

How do you know?

____

e. If the water is heated for five minutes more, what do you think the temperature will be? Malik said 120 °C. Rhianna said 100 °C. What do you think?

____

✓ Checklist

I understand.

I understand a bit.

I need more help to understand this.

Read each sentence and circle a face for it. Like this:

- I can tell the difference between boiling and evaporation.
- I know the melting point of water.
- I know the boiling point of water.

2.5 Making and separating solutions

1 Soluble or insoluble powders?

Work in a small group.

a. Plan a test to see if some powders are soluble or insoluble. Look at page 39 of your Student Book for some hints.

Draw a sketch of your plan.

b. Record your findings in the table:

Powder tested	Soluble or insoluble?

Extension

a. Using what you know about particles, explain how sugar dissolves in water.

You can show sugar particles as white balls. The water particles can be blue balls.

Use this drawing to help:

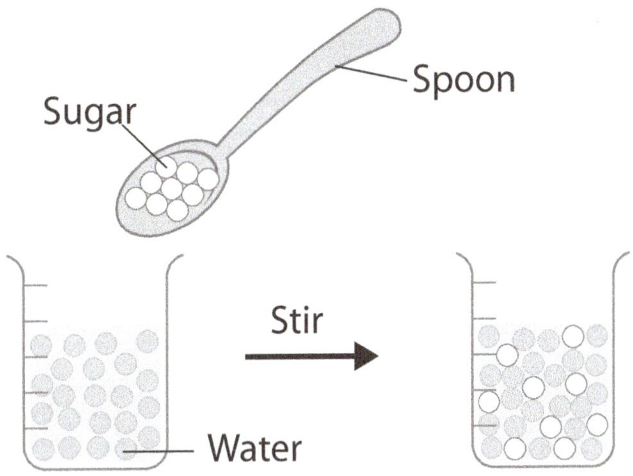

When you stir sugar into water ______________________________

____

____

____.

b. Why does sugar *seem* to disappear when it dissolves?

Sugar seems to disappear because ____________________________

____

____.

c. How can you prove that the sugar is still there in the sugar solution? Try to think of two ways.

To prove the sugar is still there we can ______________________

____

____

____.

2 Sorting coffee beans

Work in a pair.

Design a machine that can sort coffee beans into three different sizes.

Draw a labelled sketch of your design.

3 Filtering muddy water

Draw a scientific diagram of your experiment. Do not forget the labels.

Extension

Filter paper has very tiny gaps between the fibres in the paper. Look at this piece of filter paper viewed under a microscope.

Using what you know about particles, explain how filtering can make muddy water clear.

When you pour muddy water through filter paper ______________________

____

____

____

____

____.

4 Salt from salty water

Explain what has happened when there is no further change to a saucer of salt solution left on a windowsill for a couple of days.

When there is no further change to the salt solution ______________________

____

____

____

____.

Practising my science language

5 Which method gives the biggest salt crystals?

a. Will you get bigger salt crystals by evaporating the water off a salt solution quickly or slowly?

- Make a prediction.

  I think that ______________________________________

  ____

  ______________________________________.

- Give a reason for your prediction.

  This will happen because ______________________________________

  ____

  ______________________________________.

b. After observing the experiment, decide which method gave the bigger crystals.

Circle the correct answer:
evaporating slowly / evaporating quickly

Was your prediction correct?

Circle the correct answer: **Yes** **No**

Draw a magnified crystal from the samples of salt in Activity 4 and Activity 5:

Evaporating slowly (Activity 4)	Evaporating quickly (Activity 5)

Practising my

science language

6 Trouble in the kitchen

Look at the picture of Hiro mixing sand into salt on page 44 of the Student Book.

Imagine you are Hiro's big brother or sister.

Write a plan, as a series of steps, to help your mother get her pure salt back. Look at the hints on page 45 of the Student Book to help you.

Step 1

First I will ____

____.

Step 2

Then I will ____

____.

Step 3

Finally I will ____

____.

Extension

Work in small groups.

a. Which is more soluble in water – salt or sugar? Plan a fair test to answer this question.

To find out which is more soluble in water I will ____________________

____

____

____

____

____.

continues on following page …

... continued from previous page

b. Evaluate your method. Are your tests really fair? How can you improve the investigation to get more accurate results?

To make my test fairer and get more accurate results I will ________

____

____

____

____.

Checklist

Read each sentence and circle a face for it. Like this:

- I understand.
- I understand a bit.
- I need more help to understand this.

- I can test whether materials are soluble or insoluble.
- I know how to separate a mixture of materials by sieving.
- I know how to separate a mixture of materials by filtering.
- I can describe how to collect a solid from a solution.

Glossary

Fill in the meaning of these words in your own language.

boiling point

condensation/condense

crystals

evaporation/evaporate

filter funnel

filter paper

gas

insoluble

liquid

melting point

particles

sieve

solid

soluble

Glossary

solution

____

____

state of matter

____

____

water cycle

____

____

water vapour

____

____

3 The life cycle of a flowering plant

What about seeds?

Work in a pair.

a. How do you think seeds are made?

Seeds are made ______________________________

____

______________________________.

b. What do you think is inside a seed?

____

c. When did you last eat a seed?

____

d. List the different things made from seeds that you have eaten this week.

This week I have eaten ______________

____

____

____

____

____

____

____

____

____

____

______________________________.

2 What's inside an apple?

Work in a small group.

a. Describe the apple in detail.

____

____

b. Cut the apple in half from top to bottom. Draw a labelled diagram of what you see inside.

c. How many seeds are inside the fruit? ____________________

Describe the apple seeds.

____

d. Why does an apple tree grow blossom and fruit?

It grows blossom and fruit because ____________________

____

____.

Why do you think that the blossom and fruit appear at different times of the year?

They appear at different times of year because ____________________

____

____.

3.1 Monitoring plant growth

Practising my science language

1 Observing plant growth

lettuce	radish	cress
broad bean	sunflower	

Work in a small group.

a. Circle the type of plant in the box you will observe.

If it is a different plant, write its name here: ______________________

b. Answer these questions to make your plan.

- How will you grow your seed or seedling?

____

- What does a seed or seedling need to grow well? Make a list.

____

- Describe how you will make sure your seed or seedling gets what it needs.

To make sure my plant gets what it needs, I will ______________________

____.

- What do seedlings need that most seeds do not need?

____

- How will you observe and present your results to show the growth of your plant? Write a brief plan in the box. You must include some measurements you plan to make.

continues on following page …

… continued from previous page

c. Draw a table to record your observations and measurements during this unit.

Your table could have three columns. Here are the headings you could use. Fill in the missing word:

- Time since start of observations (in days)
- Changes observed
- Size of ________ (in mm)

2 Making measurements

a. Besides the height of a plant, what other measurements can you take using a ruler?

The measurements I can take are ______________________________

____

____.

continues on following page …

... continued from previous page

b. Read these two measurements and write your answers below.

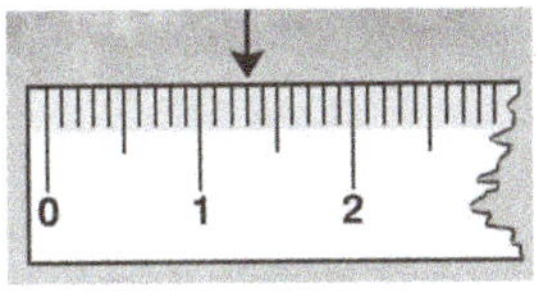

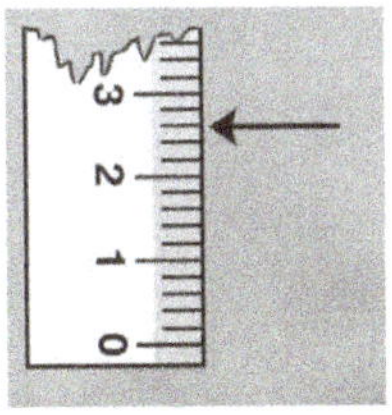

_____ mm _____ mm

Extension

A group investigates four different plant seedlings to see which grows the fastest in one week.

a. Which variables (factors) need to be controlled to make it a fair test? The group will need to keep these things the same:

____

____

b. Which type of graph can they display their results on?
Circle the correct answer: **a bar chart / a line graph**
Explain your answer.

I chose this type of graph because ___________________________

____.

Checklist

I understand.

I understand a bit.

I need more help to understand this.

Read each sentence and circle a face for it. Like this:

- I can observe and measure changes in plant growth over time.

- I know how to record and display data about plant growth over time.

3.2 Seed dispersal

1 **Numbers of seeds**

Why do you think so many fruits contain far more than one seed?

Many fruits contain more than one seed because

____

____

____.

Hint

Think about the chances of every seed growing into a new healthy plant. What might happen to a seed before it can grow?

Practising my science language

2 **'Helicopter seeds' investigation**

Work in a pair.

a. Look at the picture on page 56 of the Student Book. Write down the question you will investigate. Fill in the missing words:

How does the ______________________________ affect the time it takes the spinner to fall a set distance?

b. Make a prediction and explain it. Complete the sentences:

I think that if we make the __________________________________

bigger, then the time for the spinner to fall will get _______________.

This is because ____

____.

- What variable will you change in each test?

  ____

continues on following page ...

... continued from previous page

- What will you measure to judge the effect of changing your chosen variable?

  ____

- What variables will you keep the same in each test to make your investigation fair?

  I will keep these variables the same: ______________________________

  ____

c. Plan a method for your investigation. Do you think it will be a good idea to repeat each test? Why do you think this?

To carry out my investigation I will ______________________________

____

______________________________.

d. Fill in the gaps in this table, including any units. Then record your results as you carry out your investigation.

	Time for spinner to fall (in ______)			
	First test	**Second test**	**Third test**	**Average**

e. Look carefully at your results. How will you interpret your findings? What conclusions can you draw after your investigation?

My results show that ______________________________

______________________________.

Explain how you can improve your investigation.

To improve my investigation I could ______________________________

____

______________________________.

Extension

a. Which features of a coconut make it capable of growing so far away from the parent tree?

Coconuts can grow far away from the parent tree because ______________________________

____

____

______________________________.

b. Where do the new shoots and roots start growing from in a coconut?

____

____

c. Describe what you will find inside a coconut if you crack open its shell. Try to explain your observations.

If I crack open a coconut I will see ______________________________

____

______________________________.

Checklist

Read each sentence and circle a face for it. Like this:

- I understand.
- I understand a bit.
- I need more help to understand this.

- I can explain why plants disperse their seeds.
- I can explain four main methods of seed dispersal: wind, explosion, animals and water.
- I can identify germination as the process that follows seed dispersal.

3.3 The parts of a flower

1 Matching the parts of a real flower

Work in a pair.

Sketch and label your flower using the following words:

petal sepal stamen carpel

2 Making a model flower

Work in pairs.

a–c. Follow the instructions on page 60 of your Student Book to make a model of a simple flower.

d. In what ways are your class's model flowers different to each other?

These things are different:

____

____

Is there another model flower that is very similar to yours? Can you describe how?

These things are the same:

____

____

Extension

Close your Student Book. Try to draw the general structure of a flower. Label your diagram with the name and function of each part.

3.4 Pollination and fertilisation

1 Why do plants make pollen?

Work in a small group. Write a summary of your ideas about why insects regularly visit flowers.

Insects visit flowers because ______________________________

____

______________________________.

Extension

a. Make some notes about hay fever. What is the role of pollen in causing hay fever?

b. Use your notes to produce a booklet about hay fever for people to read in a doctor's waiting room. Make sure you mention the role of pollen.

Practising my science language

2 Acting out pollination

Work in a group of five or six. On a separate piece of paper, plan a presentation of what happens in the process of pollination. You can either:

- act out pollination as it actually happens in nature
- or make up your own story to model pollination using the ideas of advertising, rewards and the movement of things from one place to another. You can create images as part of the story.

3 Modelling the story of pollination and fertilisation

Use your flower models from page 60 in the Student Book to show how pollination, and then fertilisation take place in a flowering plant.

Describe your presentation below. Drawing pictures may help. Use a separate piece of paper if you need more space.

4 Fieldwork

Work in a small group.

After your walk around your school grounds or a local park, make a note of the plant observations you made.

Draw any fruits or seeds you found.

Extension

Work in a pair.

a. What makes each part of a flower most effective in carrying out its job? Design your perfect flower on a separate piece of paper.

b. Write labels to explain why each feature is effective.

c. Display your poster for the rest of the class to see.

Checklist

I understand.

I understand a bit.

I need more help to understand this.

Read each sentence and circle a face for it. Like this:

- I know that plants produce flowers that have male and female organs.
- I can label the main parts of a flower.
- I know what the main parts of a flower do.
- I can identify pollination as the next stage after germination.
- I can describe how insects pollinate some flowers.
- I know how seeds are formed.

3.5 Life cycles of flowering plants

1 Arrange a life cycle

In the boxes below, sort the letters from the pictures into the circular life cycle of a flower. The first letter has been done for you.

E						

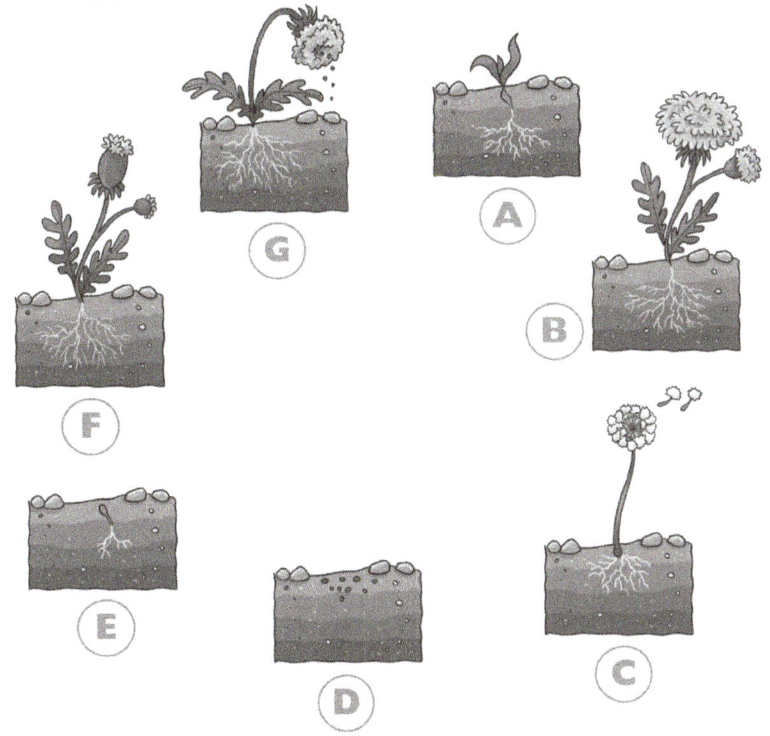

2 Label parts of a life cycle

Here is another version of the flowering plant life cycle. It is missing its labels.

Match letters A to F with the following options:

- ☐ Seed with first root and first shoot
- ☐ Fruiting plant
- ☐ Germinated seed
- ☐ Seed
- ☐ Flowering plant
- ☐ Seedling

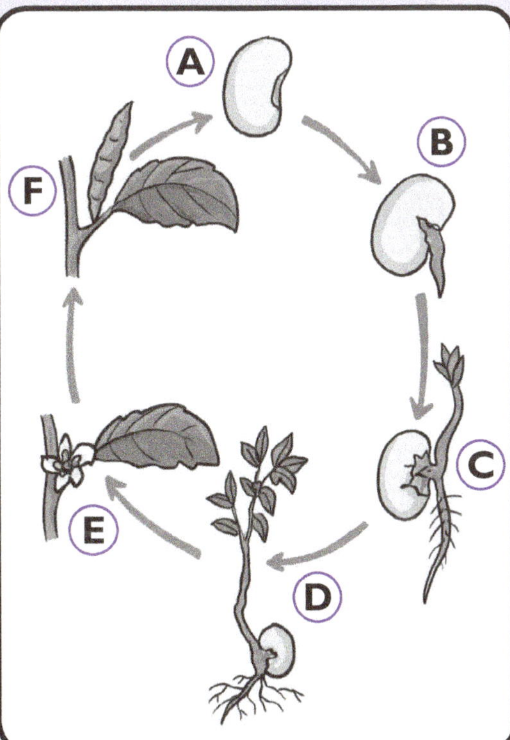

Practising my science language

3 Final report

In 3.1 *Monitoring plant growth* on page 51 of the Student Book, you set up a seed or seedling to grow throughout this unit. Look back at your table on page 52 of this Workbook.

a. What conclusions can you draw from your results?

My results show that ______________________________

______________________________.

b. Which parts of its life cycle did your plant complete?

____

c. Evaluate your investigation. If you did it again, would you do anything differently? Why?

If I did my investigation again I would ______________________________

______________________________.

This is because ______________________________

______________________________.

Extension

Mrs Edwards and Mrs Ricci each grow poppies. Mrs Edwards cuts her flowers and brings them indoors to make a nice display. Mrs Ricci likes to leave her flowers blooming in the garden. After five years, Mrs Ricci has many more poppies in her garden than Mrs Edwards.

Explain why.

Mrs Ricci has more poppies in her garden because ______________________________

____

____

______________________________.

Checklist

I understand.

I understand a bit.

I need more help to understand this.

Read each sentence and circle a face for it. Like this:

- I know that flowering plants have a life cycle.
- I know that their life cycle includes pollination, fertilisation, seed production, seed dispersal, and germination.
- I can construct the life cycle of a flowering plant.

Glossary

Fill in the meaning of these words in your own language.

carpel

dispersal (wind, explosion, animal, water)

female

fertilisation

flowers

fruit

germination

growth

insects

life cycle

male

ovum

petal

plant

pollen

pollination

reproduce/reproduction

seedling

seed production

seeds

sepal

stamen

4 Investigating plant growth

More about seeds

Work in small groups.

a. Which usually grows first, the root or the shoot?

Circle the correct answer: **root** **shoot**

Explain why.

I chose this answer because ______________________________

____

____

____

____

____

______________________________.

b. Why do seeds usually contain food stores?

Seeds usually contain food stores because ______________________________

____

____

____

____

____

______________________________.

c. Which way will the root grow in the soil?

Circle the correct answer: **upwards** **downwards** **sideways**

d. Does it matter which way up a seed is planted?

Circle the correct answer: **Yes** **No**

4.1 What makes seeds germinate?

Practising my science language

1 Do seeds need air to germinate?

Here are the results from Darya's experiment:

Factor that was changed	Number of seeds germinated
With air in bag	16
No air in bag	5

a. Suggest a conclusion for this investigation.

The results in the table suggest that ______________________________

____.

b. Why did the group use 20 seeds in each dish and not just one seed?

Fill in the missing letters in the word to complete the answer.

They used 20 seeds to make their results more r _ _ _ _ _ _ _ _.

The group left the dishes in the same place for two days. Which factors did this control?

Fill in the missing letters in the words to complete the answer.

This controlled the t _ _ _ _ _ _ _ _ _ _ _ _ as well as the amount of l _ _ _ _.

Extension

Evaluate Darya's group's investigation. Suggest why a few seeds germinated in the bag that the group said had 'no air' in it.

Some seeds might have germinated because ______________________

____

____.

4.2 Doing your own investigation into germination

1 **Which factors do you think might affect germination?**

Work as a small group.

Make a final list of the factors your group agree could affect the germination of a seed.

The factors that could affect germination are ______________________

____

____

____

____

____

____.

2 **Making a prediction**

Make a prediction about the effect of water on germination.

Explain your reasoning.

I think that ______________________

____

____

____

because ______________________

____

____

____.

Practising my
science language

3 Planning your investigation

Work in small groups.

Complete these sentences to make your plan.

a. What are you trying to find out?

We are trying to find out if ______________________________

____

______________________________.

b. What will you change in each test to find the answer?

The variable we will change is the amount of w______________ the seeds have.

c. What will you observe to judge the effect of water on germination?

We will observe whether the seeds grow a r______________ and a s______________.

d. What will you keep the same to make it a fair test?

We will keep both sets of seeds in the same p______________ to make sure the conditions are the same.

continues on following page …

... continued from previous page

e. How will you carry out your investigation? What equipment will you need?

Equipment we need to do our investigation:

____

____

Draw a diagram to show how you will set up your investigation:

f. How many seeds will you need to test?

We will test ______________ seeds, with and without water.

g. Is your plan safe?

Circle your answer: **Yes** **No**

Why should you wash your hands after handling seeds or compost?

I need to wash my hands because ______________________

____

____.

4 Completing your investigation

a. Record the results of your investigation in the table:

Conditions	Number of seeds germinated	Number of seeds *not* germinated
Without water		
With water		

b. What is your conclusion?

The results show that ____

____

____

____

____

____

____

____.

c. What type of seed did you use? ____________________

Can you be sure your conclusion applies to all types of seed?

Circle your answer: **Yes** **No**

d. How could you make your results more reliable?

I could make my results more reliable by ______________________________

____

____

____

____

____.

Extension

Isabella has an idea about water and germination.

She says, "I think that the more water you add to seeds, the faster they germinate."

a. How can you change your plan in Activity 3 to test Isabella's idea?

Here are the changes I will make to my plan:

____

____

____

b. Sketch a line graph to show what you think will happen if you carry out your new plan.

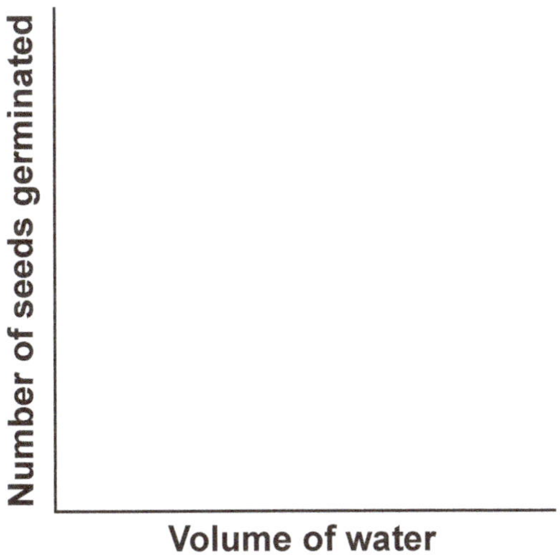

c. Explain why you chose that line on your sketch graph.

I chose this line because ____________________________

____

____

____.

5 Investigating the effect of light and temperature on germination

Work in a small group.

a. Write down your predictions for these questions:

- How do you think light or dark affects the germination of seeds?

  I think seeds germinate better when ______________________

  ____

  ____.

- What about the effect of temperature? Complete the sentence:

  I think seeds germinate better in ______________________ conditions.

b. Record your **own** group's results in this table:

Conditions	Number of seeds germinated	Number of seeds not germinated

continues on following page …

... continued from previous page

Record the **whole class's** results in this table:

Conditions	Number of seeds germinated	Number of seeds not germinated
Light and cold		
Dark and cold		
Light and warm		
Dark and warm		

c. Show the class results on a bar chart.

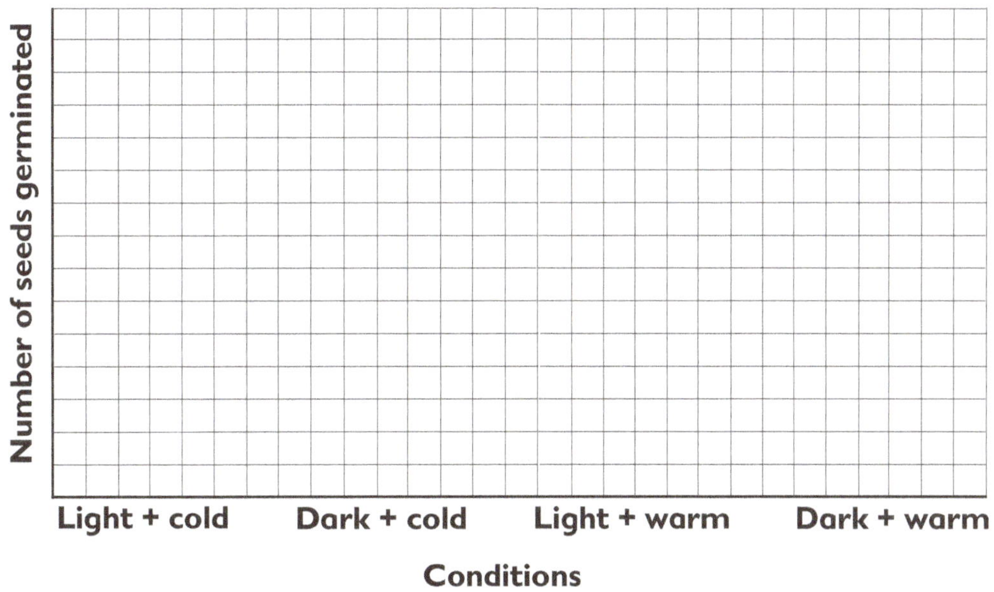

d. What did you learn from your results? Write down your conclusion.

The results show that ______________________________

____

____

____

____

____

______________________________.

Extension

You want to do the investigation again, but better than before. What are you going to change? Include as much detail as you can. Use these words in your answer.

light temperature germination fair testing reliability

To improve the class investigation I will ______________________________

____

____

____

____.

Checklist

I understand.

I understand a bit.

I need more help to understand this.

Read each sentence and circle a face for it. Like this:

- I can plan an investigation into the germination of seeds.
- I can make a prediction about germination using my scientific knowledge.
- I can carry out an investigation about germination and draw conclusions from the results.
- I can evaluate an investigation into germination.

4.3 Investigating plant growth

1 **What are your ideas about how plants grow?**

Work in a small group.

List your ideas about how plants grow:

2 **Graph decisions**

In the example on page 83 of the Student Book, temperature is shown along the bottom of the graph. If you describe the temperature as 'very cold', 'cold', 'warm', 'hot' and 'very hot', draw a bar chart.

a. How many bars do you need to draw on the bar chart? ____________

b. What do you have to do in your investigation to display your results on a line graph?

To use a line graph, I must ________________________________

____

____.

4.4 Energy for plant growth

Practising my science language

1 **How can we show that green plants need light energy for growth?**

Work in a small group.

a. What plants will you use? (You can use the cress seedlings from the previous section.) ____________________

b. How will you monitor the growth of the seedlings regularly over time in light and dark?

____

c. Design a table on a separate piece of paper to record your measurements and observations each time you check the seedlings.

d. Present both sets of your measurements (for the plant in light and in dark) on the same graph.

continues on following page …

... continued from previous page

e. Explain what evidence you used to make your conclusion about the best conditions for growing a green plant.

To make my conclusion, I ____

____

____.

f. Evaluate your investigation.

I think my investigation was ____

____

____

____.

Checklist

Read each sentence and circle a face for it. Like this:

- I understand.
- I understand a bit.
- I need more help to understand this.

- I know what green plants need to grow.
- I can plan an investigation into a factor (such as light) that affects plant growth.
- I can carry out my investigation into plant growth and draw a graph to display the results.
- I can draw conclusions and evaluate my investigation into plant growth.

Glossary

Fill in the meaning of these words in your own language.

energy

plants

germinate/germination

seeds

growth

warmth

light energy

water

5 Earth's movements

What do we already know about the Earth, Moon and Sun?

Work in a small group.

These children are sharing their ideas about the Earth, Moon and Sun.

Do you agree or disagree with the children's ideas? Fill in the table:

Things we are sure of	Things we do not really know

5.1 The apparent movement of the Sun

1 Looking at shadows

Work in a pair.

a. What object's shadow will you track the position and length of? ___________

b. What changes over the day?

During the day, the shadow ______________________________

____.

c. What stays the same all day? ______________________________

Practising my science language

2 Beijing data

Look at the bar chart. It shows the changing length of a tree's shadow.

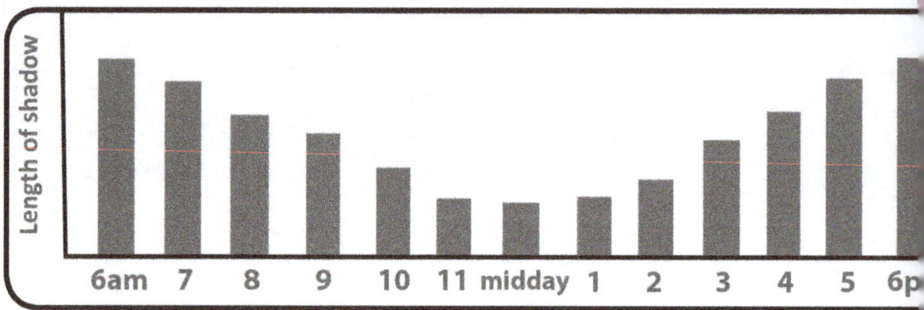

a. How many hours of daylight did the people in Beijing have on that day in March? ___________ hours

b. In Beijing, spring starts near the end of March. Summer starts at the beginning of June. What would the bar chart look like if the shadows were measured in June?

If the tree's shadow is measured in June, the bar chart ___________

____

____.

3 Sunrise and sunset in Mumbai

Here is the sunrise and sunset data for Mumbai:

Date	Sun rises at	Sun sets at	Number of daylight hours
1st March	6.42	18.48	12.06
1st June	6.02	19.18	13.16
1st September	6.27	18.36	12.09
1st December	7.06	18.06	10.59

a. The two points for March are plotted for you on the graph. The points to show the sunrise times have also been plotted on the graph.

Plot the other sunset data.

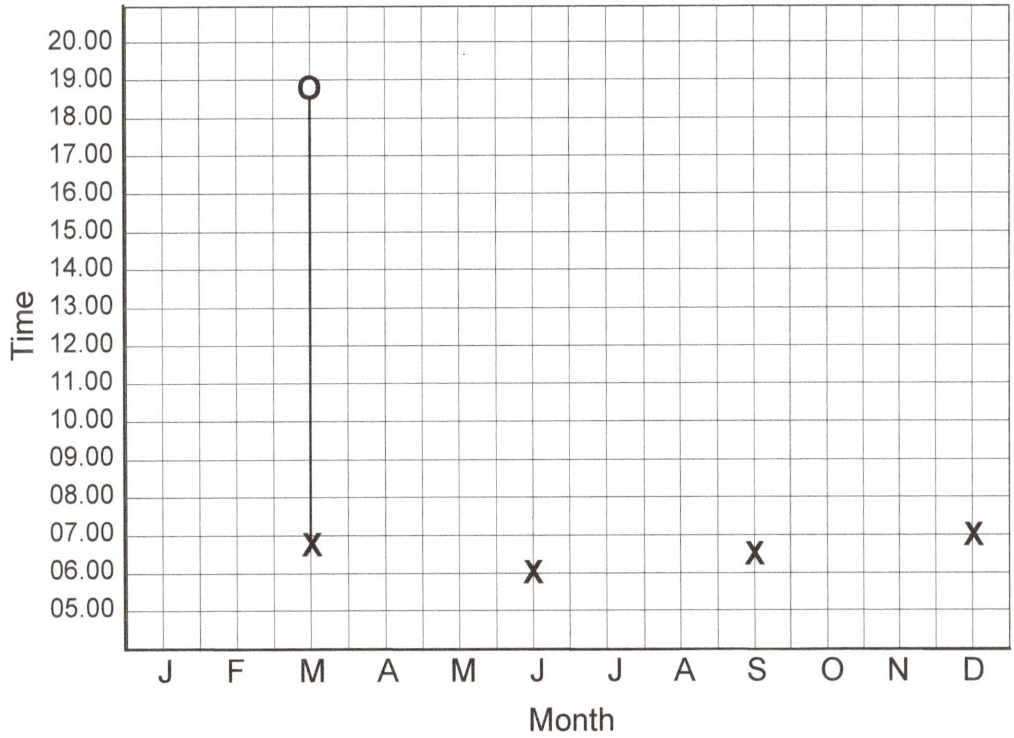

b. The vertical line shows how long a day is. Draw vertical lines between the two points plotted on the graph for June, September and December.

- When was the longest day in Mumbai? ____________________
- When was the shortest day in Mumbai? ____________________

Extension

Research the sunrise and sunset times where you live, or for a city of your choice.

a. *I am researching the data for* ______________________.

b. Fill in the table:

Date	Sun rises at	Sun sets at	Number of daylight hours
1st March			
1st June			
1st September			
1st December			

c. Plot the sunrise and sunset data for your chosen place on the graph.

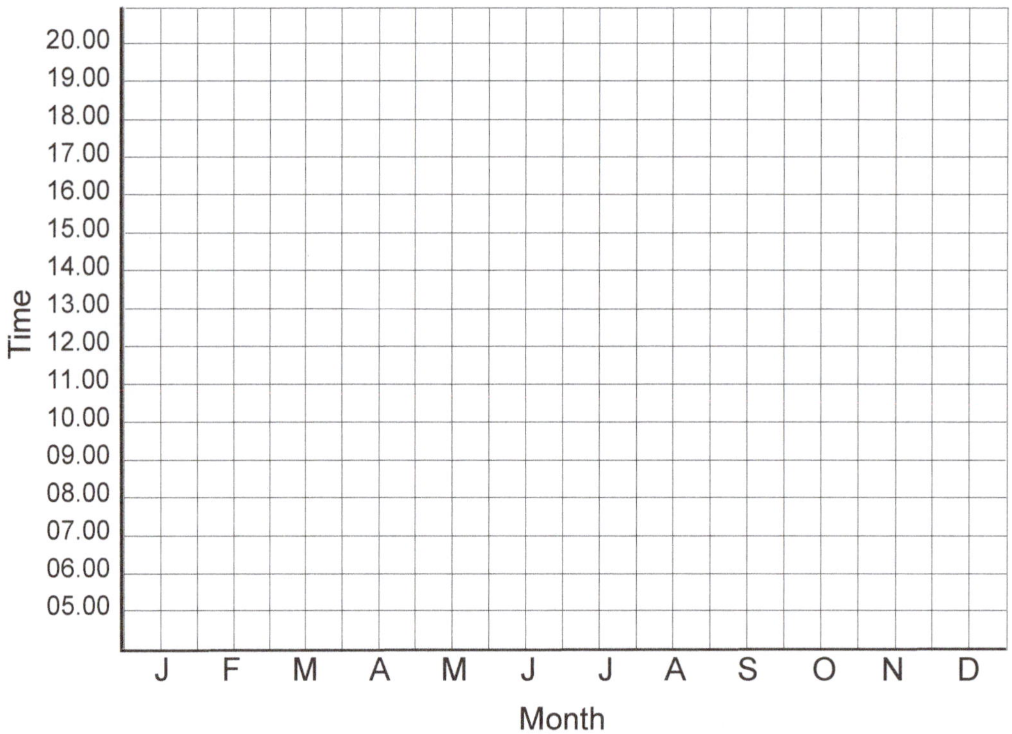

d. When was the longest day? ______________________

e. When was the shortest day? ______________________

Checklist

Read each sentence and circle a face for it. Like this:

- I understand.
- I understand a bit.
- I need more help to understand this.

- I can track the path of the Sun across the sky.
- I understand how shadows are affected by the position of the Sun.
- I can explore sunrise and sunset times.

5.2 The spinning and orbiting Earth

1 Modelling day and night 1

a. Turn your globe so the modelling-clay figure is at breakfast time, lunchtime and bedtime.

b. When the country you are in is in daylight, on which part of the Earth is it night-time? ____________________

c. How many hours does it take the real planet Earth to spin all the way round once? _____ hours

Practising my science language

2 Modelling day and night 2

Work in a small group.

Write a script on a piece of paper for a parent to explain to a 6 year old child how we get night and day. Use a football or basketball to represent the Sun and a tennis ball to represent the Earth.

Extension

a. Explain why it is useful to model the Sun as a football and the Earth as a tennis ball.

It is useful because ____

____.

b. Why is this also a poor model of the real Sun and Earth?

It is a poor model because ____

____.

Extension

Mercury spins very slowly. It takes 60 "Earth days" to spin once. Mercury takes 90 "Earth days" to complete an orbit around the Sun.

On Mercury, explain why there are only one and a half "Mercury days" in a "Mercury year".

There are only one and a half "Mercury days" because ___________

____

____

____.

3

Earth timings

Work in a pair.

Who can answer these questions about time more quickly? You will both need a calculator.

Start your timer.

a. How many seconds are there in a minute? _____ seconds

b. How many minutes are there in an hour? _____ minutes

c. How many seconds are there in an hour? _____ × _____ = _____ seconds

d. How many hours are there in a day? _____ hours

e. How many days are there in most years? _____ days

f. How many hours are there in most years? _____ × _____ = _____ hours

g. How many hours are there in a leap year? _____ × _____ = _____ hours

Stop your timer.

h. Check your answers. Add 20 seconds to your time for each wrong answer.

Who was faster?

My time: ____________________

My partner's time: ____________________

4 Seasonal differences

Work in a pair.

a. Do you live in the northern or southern hemisphere? ______________________

In which months do your summer and winter take place?

____

b. Describe the main differences in the weather between the seasons in your year.

In summer, the weather is ______________________________

____

____

____.

c. Can you explain any differences in temperature in the year? Use the diagram of the Earth and Sun on page 98 of your Student Book to help you.

The differences in temperature are caused by ______________________

____

____

____

____

____

____

____.

d. Describe how one animal is affected by the different seasons where you live.

The animal I have chosen is ______________________.

In summer, it is ______________________________

____

____.

e. How can you tell when springtime is on its way?

I can tell it is nearly spring because ______________________

____

____.

Practising my

science language

5 Modelling the orbiting Earth

Work in a pair. Describe how you and your partner can act out the movements of the Earth around the Sun.

____

____

____

____

____

____

Extension

a. Which planet has the longest day? __________

b. Which planet has the shortest day? __________

✓ Checklist

Read each sentence and circle a face for it. Like this:

☺ (I understand.) 😐 (I understand a bit.) ☹ (I need more help to understand this.)

- I can model the movement of the Earth and Sun to explain night and day.
- I know that the Sun does not move around the Earth.
- I know that the Sun appears to move because the Earth is spinning on its axis.
- I can model the movement of the Earth and Sun to explain the length of a year.
- I know that the Earth orbiting the Sun causes our different seasons.

5.3 Space science

Practising my science language

1 Questions about the Moon

Make up your own questions about the Moon. Start each question with one of the words given below. The first question for 'How …?' has been done for you.

a. **How** long does it take for the Moon to orbit the Earth?

b. **Where** ____
____
____?

c. **Why** ____
____
____?

d. **What** ____
____
____?

e. **When** ____
____
____?

f. **Which** ____
____
____?

g. **Who** ____
____
____?

2 Mix and match scientific questions

Work in a pair.

How would you approach the scientific questions in column 1 of the table? Link each question (from A to G) with one of the types of enquiry described in column 2 (numbers 1–7).

	Scientific questions		Types of enquiry
A	How does the length of a telescope affect how much it can magnify objects?	**1**	Observing, exploring and recording
B	What is the temperature on the surface of the planet Jupiter?	**2**	Researching – using secondary sources
C	How can you make your own telescope?	**3**	Fair testing – controlling variables
D	What type of star is our Sun?	**4**	Pattern seeking – making links from data collected
E	Does the size of a planet affect the distance it is found from its sun?	**5**	Using models
F	Why do planets have different lengths of day?	**6**	Identifying and classifying
G	What changes do you see when you record what happens to the shape of the Moon over a month?	**7**	Designing things to solve problems

3 Researching a space scientist

Write a brief report on the life and discoveries of a famous space scientist (astronomer). Carry out your research using the internet or reference books.

Name of astronomer: ______________________

Date of birth: ______________________

Date of death (if dead): ______________________

Country of birth: ______________________

Describe where they studied and worked:

They studied in ______________________

____

____

____

______________________.

Give a brief summary of the work they are famous for:

They are famous for ______________________

____

____

____

______________________.

Write down any other interesting information you found in your research. You can also stick in or draw a picture of the astronomer.

Practising my
science language

4 Plan your crater investigation

Plan your investigation into the effect of the speed of a meteor on the size of the crater.

a. Complete the sentence below to make a prediction and explain your reasoning.

I think that the __________ the speed of the meteor, the __________ the __________ of the crater. This is because ______________________________ ______________________________.

b. The variable that I will change in each test is ______________________________ ______________________________.

c. I will get the meteor (clay ball) to drop at different speeds by __________ ______________________________.

d. The variable that I will measure to judge the effect of changing the speed is ______________________________.

e. The variables I will need to keep the same in each test for fair testing are ______________________________ ______________________________.

f. Draw a table on a separate piece of paper to record your results. Include repeat measurements and their averages. See the sample table on page 105 of your Student Book for help.

5 Complete your crater investigation

a. Record the results of your crater investigation in the table you drew in Activity 4.

b. Draw a graph to present your results. What will you choose?

Circle your answer: **bar chart** **line graph**

Draw your graph on a piece of grid paper. Plot the average of the repeat measurements.

c. Do your results show a pattern? Circle your answer: **Yes** **No**

Write down your conclusion.

The results show that ____

____.

d. Evaluate your repeat measurements.

- Were the three repeats in each set grouped closely together?

  ____

- Are your results reliable?

  ____

Checklist

I understand.

I understand a bit.

I need more help to understand this.

Read each sentence and circle a face for it.
Like this:

- I know about the different approaches scientists (including space scientists) can take to answer questions.
- I have researched the life and discoveries of a space scientist.
- I have investigated the size of craters on the Moon and:
  - I understand the need for repeated measurements
  - I can present results in tables, bar charts and/or line graphs
  - I can decide whether results support predictions and evaluate repeated results.

Glossary

Fill in the meaning of these words in your own language.

24 hours

asteroids

axis

comets

day

discoveries

Earth

galaxies

Jupiter

Mars

Mercury

meteors

Moon

Neptune

night

orbit

Glossary

Fill in the meaning of these words in your own language.

planets

____

____

Saturn

____

____

scientists

____

____

solar system

____

____

space probe

____

____

spin

____

____

stars

____

____

Sun

____

____

sunrise

____

____

sunset

____

____

Uranus

____

____

Venus

____

____

year

____

____

6 Shadows

What do you know about shadows?

Work in a pair.

a. Can you have a shadow in a totally dark room?

I think that ______________________________

____

______________________________.

b. Can you make the shadow of a pencil longer or shorter? How can you do this?

I can make the shadow longer or shorter by ______________________________

____

______________________________.

Can you make the pencil's shadow change direction? How can you do this?

I can change the direction of the shadow by ______________________________

____

______________________________.

6.1 How do shadows form?

1 Finding shadows

a. How many shadows can you see in the picture? ________________

b. Describe where you can find five more shadows in your classroom.

1 ________________________________

2 ________________________________

3 ________________________________

4 ________________________________

5 ________________________________

c. Compare your list of shadows with another pair.

Which was the biggest shadow from both lists?

____

2 Making shadows

Work in a pair.

a. Use a hand torch to make a shadow. What shape is the shadow?

____

b. Draw your favourite animal shadow shape.

Practising my science language

3 Design a shadow puppet show

Work in a small group.

Describe briefly the story of your puppet show. Include some pictures of your puppets. Explain how well you think the puppet show works.

Extension

a. In a darkened room, shine a hand torch on to a book with a wall or screen behind it.

- What do you notice about the shadow of the book on the wall?
- Is a single, sharp shadow formed?

The shadow of the book is ______________________________

____

______________________________.

b. Explain your observations by drawing the book and its shadow, the torch and the rays of light from the whole face of the torch.

4 Explaining how shadows form

Look at the picture of Amira walking home on page 114 of the Student Book.

a. Did Amira have a shadow when she stopped under the streetlight to cross the road?

Circle the correct answer: **Yes** **No**

b. How can Amira make her shadow much larger?

____

c. How are the shadows made? Discuss with a partner then explain your answer in your own words. Use a drawing with light rays from a light source to help you.

The shadows are made by __________

____

________________________________.

Checklist

Read each sentence and circle a face for it. Like this:

- I understand.
- I understand a bit.
- I need more help to understand this.

- I know that shadows are formed when light travelling from a source is blocked.
- I can observe and explain how shadows are formed.
- I can explain shadows using the idea of rays of light.

6.2 Opaque, translucent and transparent materials

Practising my **science language**

1 Grouping materials

Work in a small group.

a. Write your groupings of the different objects in a table:

b. How did you sort the objects you were given into groups?

To sort the objects into groups, we ______________________

____

____.

2 Making your own decisions

Work in a small group.

Using a torch, test the materials you were given to see if they are transparent, translucent or opaque.

continues on following page …

... continued from previous page

Enter your results in the table:

Transparent	Translucent	Opaque

Extension

Here is a toy boat and some shadow shapes.

Circle the shape(s) it is **not** possible to make using this boat and a torch.

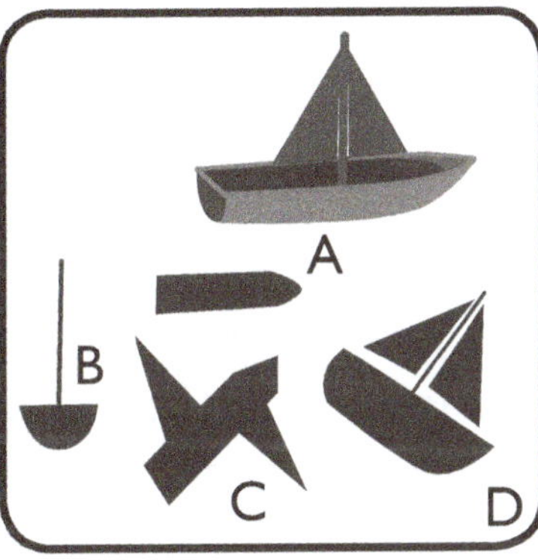

Checklist

Read each sentence and circle a face for it. Like this:

I understand.

I understand a bit.

I need more help to understand this.

- I know the meaning of the terms opaque, translucent and transparent. 
- I can investigate how to classify materials as opaque, translucent or transparent. 

6.3 What affects the size of a shadow?

1 Listing variables

a. Work in a pair. Make a list of variables that can affect the size of an object's shadow. In your investigation the object is a pencil.

The variables that can affect the size of a pencil's shadow are ______________

____

____.

b. Look at the picture on page 118 of the Student Book. Why does Sook think that Bibek is joking?

Sook thinks that Bibek is joking because ______________________

____.

c. Share your list of variables with another pair. Agree on a final list of variables that might affect the size of the pencil's shadow. After your discussion, change your list in part (a. if you need to.

Practising my **science language**

2 Planning and predicting

The question you will investigate is: "How does the **position** of a pencil affect the size of its shadow?"

a. Answer these questions to plan your investigation. Look at the image on page 119 of the Student Book to help you.

- What will be the only variable you change in each test?

  ____

- How will you measure the size of the pencil's shadow?

  ____

continues on following page …

... continued from previous page

- Name the variables you will keep the same in each test.

The variables I will keep the same are ______________________________

____

____.

b. Make a prediction about how the height of the pencil's shadow will be affected by changing its position.

I predict that changing the position of the pencil will ______________

____

____.

To help you make your prediction, draw a sketch of the light rays from the centre of the torch passing the tip of the pencil in different positions.

Wall	Pencil	Torch	Torch

- Will you need to repeat your tests to make them more reliable?

  Circle your answer: **Yes** **No**

- Is it easy to measure the height of the pencil's shadow? If not, why not? Circle your answer: **Yes** **No**

Because ____

____

____.

3 Trial run

In this trial run, you will explore how far you can move the pencil and still get a shadow to fit on your screen for measuring.

When the shadow is too big for the screen, measure the distance from the screen to the pencil.

_______ mm

4 Carrying out your plan and recording

a. Draw a table to record your measurements. Look at the examples on page 121 of the Student Book to help you.

If you plan to repeat your tests, divide the second column in the table to record each repeated test and the averages.

b. Carry out your investigation and record the results in your table.

Presenting your results

Draw a line graph to show the results from your table in Activity 4.

See page 122 of the Student Book for an example showing the labels for the axes.

Analysing your results

a. Look at your graph from Activity 5. What pattern can you see in your results? How do you interpret this pattern? Write your conclusion.

The results show that ____

____

____

____.

b. Does this agree with the prediction you made in Activity 2? Explain why, using evidence from your graph.

My conclusion ____

____

____.

Extension

Work in a small group.

Answer these questions to evaluate your investigation.

a. Did anything go wrong in your tests? If it did, say what went wrong.

In my tests ____

____

____.

b. Was anything more difficult than you thought it would be? How can you change your plan to make it easier?

Explain how this makes your investigation better.

I found that ____

____.

I will change my plan by ____

____.

This will make my investigation better because ____

____.

c. How can you improve your results? Did you take enough readings? Are your measurements accurate enough?

I will improve my results by ____

____

____

____.

d. If you repeated your measurements and worked out the averages, did you find big differences in the sets of readings? If so, explain why.

In my results I saw ____

____

____

____.

6.4 The time of day and shadows

1 **Sunny days, changing shadows**

Work in a pair.

a. What time did you start your observations? ____________

b. What happened to the shadow after 30 minutes? Write your observations.

After 30 minutes, the shadow ____

____.

c. After repeating the shadow task throughout the day, what patterns did you see in the length and position of the shadow outlines?

After repeating the task I saw ____

____

____

____.

2 **Simple sun clock (sundial)**

What time does this sundial show?

____

____

____

____

3

Making your own sundial

Draw a picture in the box of the sundial you made.

4

How does a sundial work?

Work in a pair.

In your own words, explain how a sundial works.

A sundial ______________________________

____

____

______________________________.

Extension

a. Draw the shadows of the birdbath at 12 noon and 4.30 in the afternoon below.

12 noon

4.30 in the afternoon

b. When can we not use a sundial to tell the time?

____

Checklist

I understand.

I understand a bit.

I need more help to understand this.

Read each sentence and circle a face for it. Like this:

- I can investigate how the size of a shadow is affected by the position of the object, including:
  - I can make and explain predictions of what will happen
  - I can plan how to carry out a fair test
  - I can draw a graph of my results
  - I can collect enough evidence to test my ideas.
- I know how shadows change in length throughout the day.
- I know how shadows change position throughout the day.
- I can use the Sun to tell the time.
- I can make a sundial.

6.5 How bright is it?

1

Where else is light intensity important?

Work in a group of three.

Make a list of places or events at which the intensity of light is important.

Explain why each place or event is included in your list.

Complete the sentences to give your first answer. Then add as many more ideas as you can.

Light intensity is important at

_______________________________.

This is because ____

____

____

____

____

____

____

____

____

____

____

____

____

____.

2 How bright is a light bulb (or a candle)?

a. In a darkened room, use a light meter to find out how bright a bulb or a candle is at:

- 0.5 m away
- 1 m away
- 2 m away
- 3 m away
- 4 m away.

Before you start, sketch your predicted line on the graph axes below.

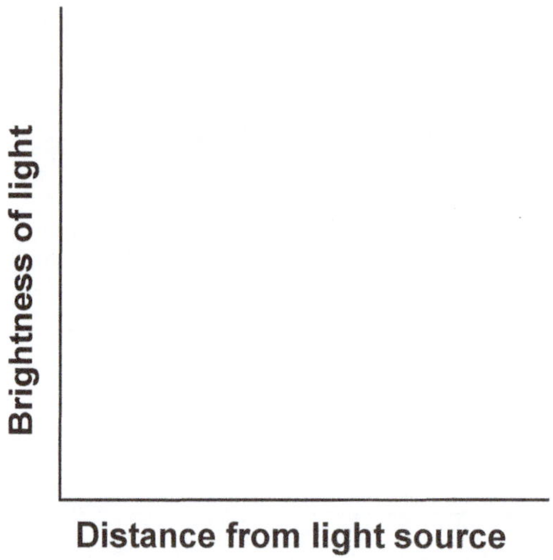

b. Compare your predicted line with a line graph drawn using the data measured by the light meter. Or compare it to the graph displayed on the screen of a computer attached to the light meter.

What do you see?

The graph is ____

____

____.

3 **How bright is our room?**

a. Measure the light intensity in your classroom with a light meter.

- Light intensity with the lights on: ____________________
- Light intensity with the lights off: ____________________

b. With the lights on, where is the darkest shadow in the room?

____

c. With the lights on, is it brighter inside or outside?

Tick one box:

☐ Inside

☐ Outside

Practising my science language

4 **How much light gets through tissue paper?**

Work in a pair.

a. What is the light intensity at a distance of 20 cm? ___________

b. What is the light intensity through a single piece of tissue paper with a light meter at 20 cm? ___________

c. Predict how much light will pass through two pieces of tissue paper. How about three pieces? Discuss your predictions with a partner then write your predictions in your own words.

Prediction for two pieces: ___________

Prediction for three pieces: ___________

continues on following page ...

... continued from previous page

d. Test up to five pieces of tissue paper. Record your results in the table:

Number of pieces of tissue paper	Light intensity (brightness) at 20 cm
0	
1	
2	
3	
4	
5	

e. Check your predictions for two and three pieces of tissue paper in part (c.. Were they accurate?

Circle the answer: **Yes** **No**

How did you make this a fair test?

To make this a fair test, I ____

____

____.

Extension

a. Plot your results from Activity 4 on a line graph.

b. Use a ruler to draw a straight line through all the points plotted. Do not join them "x to x". This "average" line is called a "line of best fit".

Checklist

I understand.

I understand a bit.

I need more help to understand this.

Read each sentence and circle a face for it. Like this:

- I know that the brightness of light in a place is called the light intensity.
- I know that light intensity can be measured.
- I can describe some places where it is important to measure light intensity.

Glossary

Fill in the meaning of these words in your own language.

block/blocked

length

light

light intensity

light source

object

opaque

position

shadow

silhouette

solid

translucent

transparent